MW00851206

ALSO BY VINCENT KATZ

POETRY

A Possible Epic of Care (with Andrei Codrescu)
Broadway for Paul
Previous Glances: an intense togetherness
Fantastic Caryatids (with Anne Waldman)
Southness
Swimming Home
One-Liners
Judge (with art by Wayne Gonzales)
Rapid Departures (with art by Mario Cafiero)
Understanding Objects
Pearl (with art by Tabboo!)
Boulevard Transportation (with photographs by Rudy Burckhardt)
New York Hello! (with photographs by Rudy Burckhardt)
Cabal of Zealots
Rooms

ARTIST'S BOOKS/COLLABORATIONS

Katz Katz (with drawings by Alex Katz)
4 × 5 (with art by Polly Apfelbaum, Leda Catunda, Philippe Mayaux, Nabil Nahas, and Juan Uslé)
Swimming Home (with woodcuts by Alex Katz)
The Dive (with etchings by Alex Katz)
Alcuni Telefonini (with watercolors by Francesco Clemente)
Berlin (with woodcuts by Matthias Mansen)
Park, Bari, Ostia (monotypes by Francesco Clemente and Vincent Katz)
Terra Fragile (with art by Francesco Clemente)
Voyages/Hyde Park Boulevard (in collaboration with James Brown)
Smile Again (with art by Alex Katz)
A Tremor in the Morning (with linocuts by Alex Katz)

AS EDITOR

Readings in Contemporary Poetry: An Anthology
Black Mountain College: Experiment in Art, with essays by Martin Brody, Robert Creeley, Vincent Katz, and Kevin Power

DAFFODIL

DAFFODIL

& other poems

VINCENT KATZ

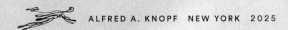 ALFRED A. KNOPF NEW YORK 2025

A BORZOI BOOK

FIRST HARDCOVER EDITION

PUBLISHED BY ALFRED A. KNOPF 2025

Copyright © 2025 by Vincent Katz

Penguin Random House values and supports copyright. Copyright fuels creativity, encourages diverse voices, promotes free speech, and creates a vibrant culture. Thank you for buying an authorized edition of this book and for complying with copyright laws by not reproducing, scanning, or distributing any part of it in any form without permission. You are supporting writers and allowing Penguin Random House to continue to publish books for every reader. Please note that no part of this book may be used or reproduced in any manner for the purpose of training artificial intelligence technologies or systems.

Published by Alfred A. Knopf, a division of Penguin Random House LLC, 1745 Broadway, New York, NY 10019.

Knopf, Borzoi Books, and the colophon are registered trademarks of Penguin Random House LLC.

LIBRARY OF CONGRESS CATALOGING-IN-PUBLICATION DATA
Names: Katz, Vincent, 1960– author.
Title: Daffodil : and other poems / Vincent Katz.
Description: First edition. | New York: Alfred A. Knopf, 2025.
Identifiers: LCCN 2024010796 (print) | LCCN 2024010797 (ebook) |
ISBN 9780525656593 (hardcover) | ISBN 9780525656609 (ebook)
Subjects: LCGFT: Poetry.
Classification: LCC PS3561.A776 D34 2025 (print) |
LCC PS3561.A776 (ebook) | DDC 813/.54—dc23/eng/20240520
LC record available at https://lccn.loc.gov/2024010796
LC ebook record available at https://lccn.loc.gov/2024010797

penguinrandomhouse.com | aaknopf.com

Printed in Canada

The authorized representative in the EU for product safety and compliance is Penguin Random House Ireland, Morrison Chambers, 32 Nassau Street, Dublin D02 YH68, Ireland, https://eu-contact.penguin.ie.

for my parents

CONTENTS

1

A SLIGHT BREEZE

DAFFODIL

If I imagine all time sequestered in the fold of a daffodil,
Close to the desire of sitting next to someone,
It's like a trip uptown and then one downtown,
And my door is open to the revenge of snow.
Clasp me as a trumpet seeks release,
I should see daydreams in eyes
All aflutter and simplified down,
The stores and all the other places we settle down to.

PULLING OUT

Next stop West Haven
We are pulling out in two minutes
We are leaving behind
We are going forward

Was something said?
What was imagined? What projected?
And then, the reality,
Always better, sharper,

Putting the day, the trees,
Into relief, giving relief
Ultimately, in a world
Of opportunities

POEM FOR DAVID MELTZER

I am listening to Radiohead on a friend's playlist

The playlist in our heads keeps playing even after you've gone

Even after you've gone, the music keeps playing

Playing in our heads, turning around, accumulating

New emotions in the hearts of new listeners

After being away in the woods for weeks

And thinking of those one loves who may not long be here

The music keeps playing in our heads, strangely

Something new keeps pulling us, coming from the new

And equally from the old, new and old are the same age

When I have the time in my head,
I can see the floor, those patches,
Strips I've looked at all my life,
Suddenly can focus there, and on
The floor beyond, also lilies and maple
Outside my window, this room I grew
In, thought, and planned, and wrote in;
What did I think, all those years, when
In bed, quiet, waiting for sleep, or
Imagining some world to come?

A SLIGHT BREEZE

A silent afternoon
Like one hundred years ago
Silent, trapped in time
Fire escape shadows

On tenement sides transfixed
An extension of steps into
Design, and clouds silent,
Flowing, only movement

A slight breeze in ailanthus
Leaf, something so quiet
Ancient in the afternoon
A bird's chewing tweaks

SPRING

I can see what was seen as professionalism
Is pure emotion

And there, where we see it, is where
We have been left, to see

How much is available, once
It has been identified, later

The margins seem to contain all
That is considered of a piece,

One left that place, but one has
Returned, trees in leaf again above

Those paths, standards upheld
At risk once again enabled

BRYANT PARK ODE

The skating rink is down
They're going to figure out how to grow grass again
A crane lurks on hidden high-rise
Grace to be born and live as variously as possible
She's an amazing intelligence
I'm lucky to have her in my life for a time
Everything is for a time

Photographing statues in the rain
Give us this day our daily ornate bronze Romanesque lamp post
Ram's head garland leafy fountain
Can you hear the fountain?

Odd hump where grass goes

ON HEARING THE STROKES OUTSIDE COMMONS

for Isaac & Oliver

Music coming down again
A simple refrain
A little mournful but then
That is the tenor ultimately
And if it's reminiscent
Of other music that too
Is a human trait
At the end we all just sit
With what we've got

KEYS AND RIPPLES

for Francesco

There comes a time when everything clarifies
You open your eyes to the day
And you are seeing someone who is there
So many departed and only one begun

Here, where it is a new day
A surface is more than a surface
It is a support and way to see deeper
In further detail the signals one sends

The body as a human landscape
The wedding ring is on the hook
Yoga extension into sky
Above home-protected animals

Love is two people meeting
Face to face and heart to heart
The famous diver changes his mind
Halfway down he doesn't want to anymore

Collections of materials, grants
Of superior intelligence
Walking through the space between
Two minds two hearts on earth

FOR JOHN

People create lives
Families occur as lives grow
Together and with separation

Drums in the park at night
And another music people congregate to
The musics mix, and the people, walking across in the dark

Rhythm comes out of the dark, bonding
People, blending them
Back in the streets, people are walking

There is a slowdown, is there no mystery, or is there?
Something different from what appears
A tendency toward life that is not darkness

A MAN

The man marginalized so distant
Right next to society
Two lovers have taken showers in tandem
Others are walking to work, meeting obligations of weather
And style, smiling to each other

Soiled from head to toe
He walks at a different pace,
Which is no pace
Takes him four minutes to walk a block

The light from inside he sees not
Nor the light as it changes the sky
His day is ever dull
He walks or stands in pain without complaint

PRESS HOTEL, PORTLAND

To be brought to a place where
Word is prime is unexpected pleasure
Its continuousness others make
Continuous gesture

It is a low light that fronts
Brusque temps, light licking
Flapping flags, a lofted, landlocked,
Lighthouse, industrious blowers

The light keeps getting brighter
And the gold atop that steeple

Along behind the houses, it comes nearer
Vast tract of sound, admitting, exonerating,
Aflood with vowel reach, internal
Stretch to other unknown.

While the path veers,
A group convenes, even one of a number,
Studies are ways of communal thought
But the sound out by the path,
Where the abandoned car lurks
In the woods, is pristine,
It hurtles among fistfuls, garlanded,
Seeming a lost irony in the bushes.

There's a light and a flow,
Prints in newly present mud.
But still the drawings of twigs beneath ice.
There's low light on an oak leaf, tan and drying out
On the ground, the ice keeps the air cool.
A huge sideways chunk of what was once a tree,
Still projecting life and mission into air.

A mission: that could be to be in touch.
"A better understanding of the peoples of the earth" (FDR)
And Roland Hayes sang Berlioz.

A talk around a table, an asking, followed by an offering.
In the offing, deference, a show to

Present, one no longer only one,
How had that happened?

Saint Arnaud, Christchurch, Twizel, moving south,
And a gathering near the fire,
Talk of aspirations, projects, sillinesses,
All a shared gold, and in some,
Ambition to know that one and one
Should coalesce by times to more than
Can be fit into magazines or books.

The snow is dark, still light in latest light.
Windows lit across are human endeavor,
They release a pattern to cold.
Then the snow is more visible, instead of less.
A wind is heard, bolsters senses of night.

The light on all those trees:
A display of brown hanging oak leaves,
The hard snow, water beneath cracking ice.
All in all, a reasonable supposition.
But to care, to converse, to research a situation;
Times have changed dramatically.
But not only for the worse —
There is common interest, and support,
There is learning, in long days and cold nights.

The light visible from these windows
Provides the content for this day's breathing.
You wonder if anyone will read anything,
And you think of those gone who won't.

Someone gets out of a car into the cold,
Icy snow piles and streaks where it melted.
A bird bath, two cars, a truck, and a white van parked.
The large house opposite holding temporary lives,
Works less temporary perhaps, sounds of
Living coming and going.
The truck and van have left.
Does anyone think it worthwhile to worry
About words, lines and commas?
Someone does, and could, even one who
Knows a greater thing perpetuates itself by
Gaining an understanding in time.

In the snow that keeps falling,
Spreading gently over ground,
In the cold that goes up the tall pines at night,
We form a number, albeit shifting,
Albeit some more than others.

Networks are superficial, break down;
Friends help you, down the road.
The help might only be a word,
But it's enough to see the light of day.

2
SPECIES

THE SNAKE

The snake dazzles in grass
She swims, hallucination
Constant shimmying
Swimming through
To beyond where
We find, there to rest
Momentarily, the fear
Abated, heart
Less tense, she again
Starts, looking, smelling
Now for foe
Now for food

THE RABBIT

for Elaine

Seen her or him or them
Hopping around lately
The hope in fear
In thrill to run
Ear fine-tuned
To danger and excitement
She or he or they
Skip up steps
Run lightning-quick
Across grass to cover

THE SNAPPING TURTLE

I

I found you on the road
By the creek
You were stolid, refusing to budge

I've gotten you to face
The edge of the road
About a meter away

But you like it here
Probably enjoying warmth
Radiating from the asphalt

From the edge you could
Slide down to the creek
And find food and safety

But you don't
You lie there, impassive
As morning wears on

2

I protect you
From passing cars, gesticulating
Waving them around

But you stay
Immobile on your patch
Of road

I hear back from Aark
Who explain snappers go
In one direction only

You face the creek
But show no inclination to move
Are you sick, or dying?

3

Finally, a huge truck comes and idles
Its roar startles you, you
Make for the edge

After consulting the drop
You move and finally
Plummet! I hear your thump!

I look and look but can't find you
So I descend some tree roots
And finally see you nestled

Next to brother rock
You two identical
Huge forms in the morning

THE TICK

The tick does not get much validation
From the human environment
Seen as an unnecessary pest, like
The mosquito

Ticks, however, like bedbugs,
Emerald ash borers, and spotted
Lanternflies, are good at what they do

Ticks present
No danger to trees
But rather a hazard to humans mainly

Unlike the emerald ash borer, responsible
For the decimation of the spectacular
Growth of ash trees across
This continent

THE MOLE

I've seen their tunnels blowing up the lawn
Near trees, humps in the grass

One day, I saw a mole
A bit bigger than a mouse
Their fur dark brown
They were stretched out on the grass
I thought they might be dead
They didn't move at all

But when I came back later
They were no longer there
So maybe they were taking some kind of outdoor siesta

I don't mind the tunnels really
The grass is beautiful
And the tunnels are small
They are mostly around
Bases of trees, out of the way

Keith found him (or her, we never found out)
She was curled up on the lawn
Barely moving, but her nostrils moved when we came closer
Later she moved to a shed
Isaac kept her company for long periods
Making sure she didn't go too far back, where she might get stuck
She moved quickly though
And he couldn't stop her from falling down a steep drop and
    injuring her leg
She was tiny but had a loud voice
And she hollered repeatedly

She moved to a protected rock
At the corner of the barn
Where she blended in with the leaves and earth

Oliver called Aark
They explained that the mother
Was probably with another fawn
And would come back at dusk for this one
They said not to touch the fawn
Her best protections are that she has no scent and is able to blend in
    with her surroundings
Making her almost invisible
One touch could leave a scent on her
That a predator might track

They said her prime predator was the fox
At night, coyotes would also be a danger, if the mother did not
    return

Later, the fawn went to another shed
Where the groundhog has its lair, with two or three little hogs
She was wedged way back under some scaffolding

We saw an adult deer, possibly the mother

At dinnertime, Oliver called Aark again, explaining she had been
    under the scaffolding
A long time and maybe couldn't get out
They advised getting her out at this time

Isaac and Oliver donned gloves and carried her out to the field
After dinner, I went for a walk
It was still light out as I walked to the field
I walked down one path next to a grove of ash and walnut trees
I came back
It was raining lightly
I took some photos of the trees at the edge of the field
I looked at the grass in the field in the lightly falling rain

THE CICADAS

Like crickets,
Cicadas will always be part of
My inner mind
Their sound so ancient
Drawing our psyches
Back down centuries' paths

Birds too, but they
Always seem to have an individual song
Cicadas join in collective hum
Rising in power as the day
Nearing its end
Seems to rise
They push and turn it
Chorus of lasting effect

Crickets provide aural carpet
Cicadas another
Crickets blanket the earth
Cicadas cry from trees

THE WATER BUG

It is enormous
Threatening
There's a desire to kill it
And a desire not to
But allowing it to go free
On the roof is also perilous

They move quickly
They fly
They are very aware
Of being hunted

Capturing it in a cup,
How much does the cup
Need to be cleaned?
We think of water bugs
As by definition filthy

But how much of
The water bug is actually
Dirty? Do we really know?

DRAGONFLIES AND FROGS

Gentle flute sound
From the radio
Air still
No cars pass

This is the time of life
That is good
It is passing and
At the same time here

SPECIES

I love this light
And the sounds of birds singing
I am a connoisseur of birdsongs
Not that I know the names of the species
Associated with the songs necessarily
But I spend a lot of time listening to their music

Two doves sit on the railing kissing
It is pecking actually, first one, then the other
They take turns, each giving quick pecks for about two seconds at a
    time
Forever it seems
Now they have stopped
And still sit there, side by side
One has turned away and may be sleeping
The other grooms herself

In the trees below the window, more birds and songs
The backyard is crazy with song
This is what I most admire about birds
And what most attracts me to them:
They seem to sing by necessity from happiness
They sing in the morning, when light touches the sky
And they are singing now, as this incredible last light lingers
In a fresh spring evening

Even here, in the depths of the city, in a backyard
Shared by several buildings, characteristic rooftops,

Brick chimneys, tar-papered parapets, stairwell bulkheads, elevator
    housings,
More and more buildings piling up in the distance,
The wail of sirens, horns, the clug of trucks, traffic, even amid all
    this, they sing

Another dove has come to perch on the fire escape

They dispute now, they are not singing precisely
Still there is music in it
There are yelps, upward yearning
And the feeling too that my desires
Are included,
Out now on the street with cars and songs,
What are they saying?

Now a high-pitched pinnacle, repeating,
Differentiates itself from the lower, rhythmic, crunching —
It becomes a counterpoint
Do they hear it as such?

II

Two sets of tapping, from opposite sides,
The morning song near the kitchen over,
Now move into caw and percussive rattle of actual day,
Thrilled by sudden trill and melodious grace-note rise-drop

Over tall grass and staggered Queen Anne's lace,
Two tiny moths pursue each other in circles,
As though in love — maybe they are

In the end of day, a sloping, sweeping song,
A little tired, never without energy, never without hope
It is the tired singing of a day well spent, a day
Spent doing the things one knows how to do
That one knows are the right things, that do not
Invade anyone's privacy, or infringe upon their rights
In fact, it may be that these activities help

III

The young women have to take the places of their mothers,
Early, before their time, but somehow they do it, as
They do everything, non-violently

Majestic, highly intelligent, they proceed, and gather,
Sometimes even making it to the ocean, in their search
For the depths of water

3

AGAIN ON THE AVENUE

A NEW YORK SONG

A New York night
Slightly melancholy
An air of horns
Two young women walk
In skirts and tops
Everything light

A quietness even
In people dining outdoors
At restaurants

The next day fresh breeze
Music coming through
From somewhere
You sit at your local
Café outdoors
And drink coffee
And think

You think about
The different kinds of
People you are seeing
You feel the breeze around
Your arms and back and you
Are any age suddenly are
Again in that place you
Were when world was fresh

The different types
Within that vast continent
Playing that game last night
That ultimate expression
Of skill and strength
And speed and style

Types or just
Individuals
That artist harbored
Photographs of
Just people
No one thinks
Themself a type

PANDEMIC PARK POEM

I've always wanted to sit on this bench
Now is the perfect temperature and time
Hardly anyone in the park this Thursday evening

The scent of marijuana being smoked
By two gentle souls on a nearby bench
Wafts over, creating a congenial vibe
Two young women huddle together on the grass
Their dinner in a paper bag nearby
They must be sharing something
That can't be shared by anyone else

Two squirrels chase each other down a slender trunk
In a burst of speed
Are they in love or fighting over food?

There's a guy shirtless in shorts on his phone
And someone crashed out on the bench next to him
A trio has spread out a blanket, taken off masks
And is beginning to share their dinner

More people coming in, drizzle starting to fall lightly
Two buildings stand out in the distance

A wetness on the ground
Puddles, and I can't reach you
Except through this music
Which pulses so long ago
Is revived in synapses anyone
There or not can transfer
Across fretboard and key

Sound understated implode
Disjunct of schedules
To crawl out of pit
A delicate glance downtown
River nearby an assurance
Light, moments that add up
I assure you intense joy

Riding down the avenue
That building stands low
As present reminder
Gift in an afternoon I take
The time to write this others
Speak or work around depth
To bottom park in other tongue

Light leaking down fresh
Again at the park where
That meeting took place

Others still walking a season
Passed expression in gait
And resistance to accepting
Vault innocuous determinant

MONDAY

for Audrey

There's such a perfect light suddenly
A perfect air
And Nels Cline is going crazy
Over incessant pulses

The low western light
Illuminates a bicyclist
And people waiting in distance
To send packages
Here and there, it's time
To send something somewhere

AWARE OF FACES

Aware of faces not just walks
The sounds in one's ears
Trumpet scrapes grime off
Bass humps in social bliss
Then there's that strange
Sound of human endeavor

They were dancing over there
In a sweet circle of abandon
Then five came over here
One changed her shirt
They lay down and smoked
And hugged all different colors

Screen grid or water?
Mind travels out but
Can't move past rain
Accumulating in front
Of buildings and roofs
The sound of it she said
To listen to then sirens
Occupied space inside
Our heads we laughed
That's the quiet sound
We thought to hear
Looking out is only
Sound a low rumbling
That is always there
Always beneath us
All our lives, wherever
We find solace, quiet
Or the brightness that
Shocks, I love that hum
Continuous connecting
Persons distant country
City imagination one
Consistent hum even
Against whatever points
At us, pulls recognition
Apart, desolate query
To fail, this system
Minute within celestial

Sphere, but people
Relish causing pain
I want to walk now
Feel rain on my clothes
And skin, feel these
Same paces, path
I know from one house
To another, or only
To the river, or only
The avenue, place
Where rain connects
People's walking urge

The March equinox
Precesses slowly westward
Completing one revolution
In 26,000 years
Here on the sidewalk
People sit in squalor
Limp and wonder
What will happen when
It finally gets cold

Solar noon
Perplexes bodies
Jam and try distance
We measure as a "day"
From behind others
Appear as one we recognize
From form and hair

Thinks about a time
Some months in the future
Will he live to see it?
Will we?
We are bound by
Our proclivities
And our sense of
What is right

The meridian

But now a shift to
Simple piano and violin
And why that is able
To penetrate so deeply
The scratches of an early
Recording, unity of purpose
Emotions without sentimentality

It's going to be a crazy day, but I'm up for it.
I'm going to wait because she likes it when I wait.
It sets up the right intensity.
And the day is not crazy at all, but calm.

CRESCENT MOON

All the way the moon accompanied me
I tried photographing it, but that was just in jest
Instead, I just looked, admired its high, long crescent
Keeping all of us company, protecting, for all we know,
Most remain unaware of its presence

Somehow it allows those two young women to pose
Their friendship for the photographer set up in this little plaza
Almost night but he's got a portable lighting tripod
Willing subjects appear to his lens

Later, in the park again, the smell of marijuana comforts
In the gentle night bent electric guitar notes
Of another evening in a different park
Mice race by, the eye drifts up, beyond the arch,
To apartments, some bright, some dim, some dark,
For once, one knows what goes on in them
That it's nothing more than what one has

TODAY'S RETURNS

I want to take this street
The light bursts into applause

A prayer above Beekman Street
Odd little place, the light above

Alive, clinging, a prayer
To the hope all is not dead

Permanently in the desire
To fluctuate, as returns, or

What they mean, do

NUTATION

I sleep in a black t-shirt, which I take off
At some point during the night
I wake to the sounds of heat pipes
And doves cooing outside my window

MAY POEM

On Fifth again
Light and space and time enough
Whatever the circumstances
Music providing key and lift
I have to remember everything
Those who remember me
Then forget it all
In the zone
Between 23rd and 14th
It's not about buying
But rather about feeling the air

Such a beautiful cold light
Did I live in that building once?
Where was Max's?
The back entrances of banks
And the Metropolitan Building
Architectural detail Fitzgerald
May have passed out on

A daguerreotype of a boy
Displaying astronomical instruments
Meatyard's Zen dissolutions
Underwater nudes
A self-portrait as a hand with a pencil
William Blake's fiery confrontation
Once thought to be Elijah in his chariot
Now thought to be God admonishing Jesus
A red-haired nude with small breasts and green eyes,
Litho by Edvard Munch
A Piranesi architecture
A large Rembrandt print of darks and shallows
A clear-cut Degas etching of a child's face
The large van Gogh corridor at the asylum
Then his wall of paintings
The garden in spring
The cypresses
Rousseau's lion eating a hind
Gauguin's first painting in the Marquesas:
A native vision of a Madonna standing with Child
While the yellow angel seems to be hiding its
Bretagne credentials
A Cézanne hillside with houses requiring Cubism
A small Vuillard corner of a table
Pollock's internal and external dimension
Rothko's smoky haze

A large Twombly in passing in mind
A large Nevelson black assemblage
Like an Egyptian temple
A quirky, feisty Elizabeth Murray
Humps in a field by Pat Steir
Al Held's awkward imagination
Vivacious goldfish in Jennifer Bartlett's pool of hours
A large Susan Rothenberg of Galisteo Creek
Strange ornery beings populate above
Guston's reclining self
A stone Modigliani head and reclining ecstasy
Marsden Hartley insignias
The hall of torsos and Rodin's burghers
And at the very beginning
Red-figured vases depicting
Two well-dressed youths
Dionysos and a sophisticated satyr
Figures curving up the curve of the vessel
Seafood in a large platter designed
To hold much of it

I've arrived at this spot
A rocky outcrop with two cherries in bloom nearby
And the entire park is blooming, finally
With that pent-up energy that says
Life can begin again, even that life
From so long ago, other springs with other adorations
The desire to move up and through whatever is happening
To some higher state of mind
Shared possibly with one, or a group, that
Would be determined later
A glowing desire filling the heart
And other bodies nearby similarly
Involved, in books, with kids, or each other, the telephone

Peeling off layers
And turning, the pressure taken off the squatting ankles,
One sits facing the sun now
Birds making music, a little dog yaps occasionally
People sit in sun or shade

I try to feel the smell of earth that is eternal
Or the breeze that blows again in this day
Even with so much suffering going on
Facing the future, feeling what could be given there, or found,
To partake of this opening of feeling, this spring

CITY BIRDS FLYING

Among the ugly new buildings I've come to like,
I've been seeing, for a few days now,
A strange and beautiful phenomenon:
Birds, pigeons I assume, like to circle within their blank spaces.
Whether for air current, flying bugs they can eat, convivial exercise,
    whatever,
They go there and add charm to these harsh, uncaring façades.
Other birds fly here too, gulls and others,
Here near the river, they also add glory and grace to the view.
And now, my friend, my buddy, my pet, my dove
Has returned and sits on the fire escape railing out my window,
A light breeze ruffling his feathers.

Three men on an elevated platform
Point a building face on Third Avenue
Above Lunetta Pizza
Garbage is hauled and deposited
Into a dumpster
Gramercy Park adorned in yellow
Flutters in the breeze this cold day
Last month of a long year

A LITTLE LIGHT FOR ADA

I've got a lamp
I'm keeping on
For the sanity
Of this country

Not one cloud
Today bright blue
Shatter on branches
A fulsome light

Up but already
Going down shadow
Stretch these avenues
And park façades

Since childhood
With new friendships
Now car ride here
And there to doctor

Later, dark already,
Light still on, I'll see
A writer's family on
Island, siren night

The first one was she was going to a place
And even there she was happy, she was received

The second was in the past, she was going
To a place there too, and she was happy

4

ONCE IN
A FIELD

ONCE IN A FIELD OF FLOWERS

They sit in a field
Surrounded by daffodils
Smiling, looking, tumbling
Ostensibly they are posing
But in effect they are being
Nature as it affects their
Being together in this moment
Of their youth together

In that, they are primal
Reminders of how we animals
Are all together in a moment
Before it gets taken away
Or we choose to move
From it, but now
We feel a vibration
From the earth

We are sitting on it
You can see earth, and one
Is upside down, his head touches
Earth, waist bridges up
How can everyone be
The same age? Their long
Hair of their time, their jeans
And t-shirts symbols of an age

Uncertainty caught there
A moment ago
Forty-three years suddenly
Nothing, that perfect time
They are together, can they
Gather that? Make something
From it, someone, take time
To be free from it?

A NEW POEM

I want to write a new poem
That isn't like the old ones
This new one will speak
With a voice that comes
In sounds she has found

I want to take longer now
Not be only a moment's
Graph, but really work
And chisel, take apart,
Remove and elide

This is actually okay,
Not chiseled, can't
Be, just the same
As always, written on
The spot, desire to get it

Down is the thing, not
From fear, but desire
Crossing the Celtic Sea
Not far from Nuuk,
Close to somewhere

COMING INTO LEAF

A big hubbub coming from the grove
Birds excited at first glimpses
Of spring flowers and worms
On the wet ground

The grove exists, it is a thing
Between fields and pastures
But it doesn't have to exist
One has to work to maintain it

THERE WAS AN INCREDIBLE LIGHT YESTERDAY

There was an incredible light yesterday
And there's one this morning too,
Cooler today, finally autumn, which has
Been hinting its appearance,
Has arrived, and it is welcome
The clouds stretch in newfound ways across the sky
And are unphotographable
Cirrus textures, long strands of ice crystals,
Are fibers in the sky's body
They act against the sky's backdrop
And simultaneously are an essential part of it

AN AIR OF MEMORIES

An air of memories
Of garments decades
Guarded against pain
Forthcoming at moment
The day holds nothing back

THE BUILDING, IN THE VERNACULAR, COMMENTS ON THE ART

The building, in the vernacular, comments on the art
Not the other way around

Much later, colder now, in the park,
The afternoon was so fresh,
Now it's the end of the day

I sit on a cement bench
Where someone just got up

And feel the warmth he left behind

PIAZZA FARNESE

for Rob

It's raining
We're fifth for takeoff
We roll slowly by Jamaica Bay
A thin strip of land separating
Us from the water
The land is marked with old wooden slats
And now we're off

Pavane pour une infante défunte
Plays through headphones drowning
Out the litany of imagined achievements nearby

The lemon peel makes it real
In my glass of Campari I'm home again
In this piazza because tourists are invisible
And denizens continue to live, drink coffee, read at tables
While clouds evaporate and light hits the front

PIAZZA S. MARIA DELLA QUERCIA

The murky light green rolls
Flickers in summer light upon it
A long black chain hangs from a high embankment
A single scull languidly plies
Gargantuan bridge foundations

A great breeze from a pale yellow
Gently, an animal lay in its midst
Content to die or perhaps
Simply to wait another night

The evening is preparing itself again
The tables are set, the glasses upside down
Two people sit near the door, smoking and talking
The bells always hypnotize me, and the light

AT THE BEACH

Light worked all day on the mountain.
The day takes a certain effect on faces.
By the end, colored by day's affections,
They take on a specific knowledge.

Different kinds of bodies, all day,
They do not leave their owners.
The body during the day is worked.
By night, it is allowed to relax.

The sun has a force that feels endless.
Though life does not, the sun
Goes eventually behind the mountain.
Colors become surprisingly bright.

The mountain was the thing
That all day seemed monstrous,
Beautifully imposing, but now is flat,
As all time is suddenly none.

Rocks thrown by gods in combat
Have landed, threatening to occlude the road
The road out, *exodos,* the end of the road
The way fish shimmer and bring
Things to a conclusion, a focus,
A certain shine in the church
That was a gallery, a focus of faces
Intellectual laughter, and then exhaustion,
But still morning, the setting up
What is necessary, even if it will also
Be necessary to take it down each evening,
A continual setting up and breaking down

Olive trees down below like soft hair
Backed by dark green cypresses
Spiking up the hill toward the church
The breeze blows a scent of lavender
Graffiti on the stones, kilometers above the sea
Two motorcycles ride past
The little cats wait for closing time
Houses twinkle across the bay

A DANCE OF LONELINESS

A dance of loneliness
You dance as you feel it

The old flowers wait for us
And the music encompassed in the stones
Marble from Penteli is the best
It was like an imitation of the sky
The wind up here is terrific
The protagonist is always Athena
The entrance was always in the east
You only get to go around once

FLYING BACK

for Vivien

The mountains rise outside the window
As the plane whistles and slowly traverses the tarmac
I don't want to leave those mountains
They got inside me somehow
Their rocky nature
And the people who grew from that

LINCOLNVILLE MOTEL

1

Two overturned wheelbarrows
Two rakes and a shovel
A panoply of silence
Sun coming up above the treeline
A good honest cup of coffee
A selection of books for your perusal
And don't forget the LPs

2

A pure light, a pure haze
And the air is light
A little cooler than yesterday
Crow caws, Sally, the Golden Lab,
Says goodbye to me silently
She knows I'm going, knows I'll be back
Sad for a moment, now she
Bounds up, looking for her ball and Alice,
Who is outside
Someone comes in for a coffee in a robe
The cars roll by in back of it

OVER THE BRONX

for Gerard

We're heading north
Over Manhattan
Slightly obscured
By clouds

We see the Harlem River,
Then Inwood, which
Comes archetypally to me
In dreams

Now we're heading west
Only clouds and
The smell of coffee
And bananas

The Bronx, where
My earliest
People came from,
Is far away

A lake below surrounded by houses
A spotty cloud table hovers in between
Rectangular portions of the plains
Interrupted by remains of forest
Cloud-shadows static on flatness

Closer to the lakefront
Fewer rectangles, more trees
Some color shifting in the leaves
A classic sensation that is somehow eternal
In the autumn land this far
From any ocean

CHICAGO

It is so great to see the shadows of buildings
On the lake
Light from the west peeks through spaces
Between buildings
Striping others between here and the water

Some like Art Deco towers, cozy tower apartments
Illuminated towers, what goes on in those rooms?
Others modernist paradigms
One of the most famous, black in its narrowing
Close enough to touch

Out there, a sailboat earlier,
Now a more stationary craft
And two approaching lines
(One looked like a tower from this angle)
Are two breakwaters, protecting the beach
With a small space between their reaching arms
For a boat to pass within

Cinnamon is the classic taste
And it has traveled throughout history

IT IS NOT EXPLICABLE IN LOGICAL TERMS

It is not explicable in logical terms
But only in the terms of love, which is not logical

THERE'S A KIND OF LIGHT I WANT TO GRASP

There's a kind of light I want to grasp
Up there above the avenue and

Today is there time for love?
Two people walk by hand in hand

A song one loves is in the air

I'LL TAKE YOU TO THE MAT

I'll take you to the mat
Because I love you

You don't get off that easy

5
FOR
LOVE

FOR LOVE

Everybody's looking for love
And hopefully finding it

If they do find it
They're probably finding

It's difficult to keep
Or maintain

It keeps shifting
Changing what it is

3 SONNETS

for Margaret

I

A stroke across space
Destroying distance
Those people spent time
Weighed on heads behind
Music lifted in halls
Opera shared recalled
And today a dull sun
Brightening is all again
Where love patters,
Somehow remains, fast
Against shutters flies
Wayward, clouds the only
Action, mind still finds
Where to swim in sky

2

Pure purchase on building
Side, the day of the new moon,
Time no longer holding
Me in any place, walking home
Last night felt a change,
Nothing different, but not
The same, still feeling that
Days later, all day buildings
Disappearing into mist,
A feeling of calm in their
Disappearance, sky still grey
Another day, but mottling,
Tending toward that complex
Hue, bright blue and white

3

Clouds at the table hover
Blanketing light above tower
While to left, blue emerges
Pushes itself resistlessly eastward
Rain also is coming now, a hit
At skylight and window, sky
Meanwhile affected, changing,
Clarity in building face, tree
Projecting spring's grey welcoming
Chill, an amazing cloud today,
Flurry of them sitting, behind,
Sky bursting, throwing off
Memory, a pure bright white
Pulling open with blue to the left

VERNAL EQUINOX

The very first day of spring
I am trying to figure everything out
Or something

It turns out I can't
So I just listen
To the piano music

Dvořák's Poetic Tone Picture
For spring
And think of someone

Doing yoga, looking out sliver
Of window, see clouds moving

Now blue is curling in, the way
Hair curls around limbs and

Limbs curl, ultimate sunlight
Cuts colored fabric, graces

Building's rise into our history
Still swim in later river light

FACES AND WINDOWS

I want to be alone
In this trance of lines

I don't want to reveal
Too much of myself

I'm alone among
These moving images

A TAN LISTENING IN TREES

A tan listening in trees
And now it's dark already, quiet
Debating whether to drive back
Tonight or in the morning
There is something scary
In each proposition:
To be far, and to come close
To walk streets we walked

THERE'S ALWAYS SOME CAR IN MY WAY

There's always some car in my way
This sunny day, heading down the river
Bombarded with people and streets
The museum, the trees growing
The lower streets taking me closer and closer
My favorite piers where I walked
And want to walk again

The tennis courts, and then below
The heart of all my feelings
My wanderings to find something
Together with someone

Bike riders, soccer fields, walks
Out toward the river

The moon embraced by mist
Hovers on a wet backdrop
The hours' arbitrary measure
Of a space we both inhabit

A BEE ON THE ECHINACEA

A bee on the echinacea
Thunder on the rumble
Golden down on sunset
Grass, last whistles, rest

WALK BESIDE YOU

I want to walk beside you
In this weather we could
Just walk anywhere, start
Here on this broad sidewalk
Then move to smaller streets

TWO CLOUDS

I saw these two clouds
And I wanted to see them with you
They were particular clouds
Almost exploding in a bright sky
Now the entire sky is covered
And it is windy and cold

ACKNOWLEDGMENTS

The following poems first appeared in the publications listed. The author is grateful to the editors.

Border Crossings: "Keys and Ripples," "Bryant Park Ode," and "Church of the Koimesis."

Free Verse: "Pulling Out," "Press Hotel, Portland," "Dark Star," "Rain," "Today's Returns," and "Two Clouds."

Hanging Loose: "Another Sunday," "City Birds Flying," and "Over the Bronx."

Journal: "Aware of Faces" and "Crescent Moon."

Live Mag!: "A stroke across space" from "3 Sonnets" and "Faces and Windows."

New American Writing: "Meridian" and "Things We Saw at the Met."

Peripheries: "For John."

R&R: "Daffodil," "Chicago," "Pandemic Park Poem," and "The Rabbit."

"Poem for David Meltzer" and "The Highway" were written at Yaddo. The author thanks Yaddo for its support.

A special thank you to Deborah Garrison for her perceptive and thoughtful guidance.

A NOTE ABOUT THE AUTHOR

Vincent Katz is the author of the poetry collections *Broadway for Paul* (2020), *Southness* (2016), and *Swimming Home* (2015) and of the book of translations *The Complete Elegies of Sextus Propertius* (2004), which won a National Translation Award from the American Literary Translators Association. He is the editor of *Black Mountain College: Experiment in Art* (2002), and his writing on contemporary art and poetry has appeared in *Art in America, ARTnews, The Brooklyn Rail,* and *The Poetry Project Newsletter.* As curator of the "Readings in Contemporary Poetry" series at Dia Chelsea from 2010 to 2021, Katz edited the anthology *Readings in Contemporary Poetry* (2017). He lives in New York City.

A NOTE ON THE TYPE

The text of this book was set in Sabon, a typeface designed by
Jan Tschichold (1902–1974), the well-known German typographer.
Based loosely on the original designs by Claude Garamond
(ca. 1480–1561), Sabon is unique in that it was explicitly designed
for hot-metal composition on both the Monotype and Linotype
machines as well as for filmsetting. Designed in 1966 in Frankfurt,
Sabon was named for the famous Lyons punch cutter Jacques
Sabon, who is thought to have brought some of Garamond's
matrices to Frankfurt.

Composed by North Market Street Graphics
Lancaster, Pennsylvania

Printed and bound by Friesens
Altona, Manitoba

Book design by Pei Loi Koay